20 Minute Finger Food & Starters

Acknowledgements

Alison's Choice for dried fruit, nuts and seeds.

Benniks Poultry Farm, Buller Road, Levin for RSPCA approved barn-laid eggs.

NZ Asparagus Council and **The Tender Tips Company** for fresh asparagus.

Pandoro for delicious fresh bread.

Regal Salmon for Regal Smoked Salmon Slices and Regal Wood Roasted Salmon.

William Aitken Ltd for **Lupi** olive oils, infused olive oils and balsamic vinegar.

Thanks to the following Wellington stores, **Freedom, Moore Wilson's** and **Theme**, who provided the beautiful tableware used in the photographs. Specifically this was from:

Freedom: Placemat page 5, woven box & coasters page 8, woven tray page 19, wire basket & glasses page 20, blue jug & glasses page 27, patterned glasses & placemat page 31, table runner & vase page 33, table runner & glass page 37, placemat & glasses page 40, jug page 49, table runner & glasses page 57.

Moore Wilson's: Glasses page 15, jug & glasses page 33, plates page 57.

Theme: Wooden board & knife page 8, fondue burner page 11, glass bowls page 20, tablecloth, succulents, salt & pepper shakers page 31, plates page 33, tablecloth page 35, plates page 43, succulents page 49.

About This Book

We know from experience how hard it is to think of something interesting but easy to serve to friends for a snack with drinks, or while chatting and relaxing before a meal.

We know too, that we are not alone with this dilemma – we've often been asked if we would please write a book on this topic, and now here it is! We have had a lot of fun putting our ideas together and testing them on our friends and families!

Whatever the occasion, whether you are serving pre-dinner snacks (for two or three) or organizing food for a 'happy hour' after work (for twenty or thirty), we're sure you'll find something suitably tempting here. Even the most conservative eaters will usually try a bite-sized sample of something unusual, even though they wouldn't consider the same thing as a meal. Similarly, you may find as we have, that those who 'live on the edge' food-wise may be excited and grateful for an offering as traditional as an asparagus roll.

Make just one of these recipes to serve to a few friends, try three or four for a larger group, or make an interesting selection to enjoy as a tapas-type meal.

Don't worry if you've made more than you need – refrigerated leftovers make great additions to lunch boxes, and wonderful midnight snacks!

If speed is a real issue enlist the help of a friend – it's always quicker and easier (not to mention more fun) to have a second set of hands – this way one person can form meatballs or wontons while another tends the stove.

It is always hard to know exactly how long it takes someone else to prepare food. We know these recipes well, and know they can be made in 20 minutes or less (barring distractions by the phone, kids, etc.). When you try a recipe for the first time, however, it may take you considerably longer than it will after you have made it a couple of times – persevere and you'll be surprised just how fast many of these can be made.

This said, here are a few tips to help you speed up preparation:

- Read your recipe and check what you already have, before you go shopping. Take the recipe (or recipes!) you plan to cook when you go shopping – just pop this little book in your bag!
- Read the recipe from beginning to end, before you start.
- Get out all the ingredients you need and arrange them in the order in which you will use them.

We hope you'll find these recipes useful and enjoy them as much as we do!

Happy cooking,
Simon Holst & Alison Holst

Hot-Smoked Salmon Pâté

This delicious dip has the attractive colour and appealing flavour of hot-smoked salmon. It may be used as a popular spread, too.

FOR ABOUT 1½ CUPS:

100–150g hot-smoked salmon
250g carton cream cheese
2 Tbsp lemon juice
1–2 Tbsp capers
1–2 Tbsp horseradish sauce
  (optional)
about 2 Tbsp chopped parsley,
  dill or chives
salt and pepper to taste

Put the salmon, cream cheese and lemon juice into a food processor and process until well mixed but not completely smooth. Add the capers, horseradish (if using) and the chopped herbs, and process, just enough to mix.

Season to taste then cover and refrigerate until required.

Serve spread on crusty bread, crackers, etc., or as a dip for vegetable crudités.

Smoked Fish Pâté

Inexpensive whole sides (or fillets) of hot-smoked fish from the supermarket deli or fish department make interesting pâtés. Buy about twice the weight of fish that you need.

FOR ABOUT 1½–2 CUPS:

200g hot-smoked* mackerel,
  kahawai or other fish
  (weighed after preparation)
125–250g cream cheese
2–3 gherkins, roughly chopped
1 Tbsp gherkin pickling liquid
1 Tbsp lemon juice
Tabasco or other chili sauce
1–2 tsp tomato paste (optional)
about ½ tsp salt

Remove and discard all the skin and bones from the fish sides or fillets. (Freeze extra fish for later use.) Purée the fish in a food processor with as much cream cheese as you like until thick and fairly smooth.

Add everything else and process until gherkins are finely chopped. Taste and add more salt if you like. If serving in a bowl, sprinkle with paprika for extra colour, if desired.

Serve on crusty bread, crostini, etc., or with raw vegetable crudités. Refrigerate left-over pâté for three or four days.

Herbed Chicken-liver Pâté

This easily made, smooth and creamy mixture is the most popular pâté we have ever made. Refrigerate leftovers for three to four days.

FOR ABOUT 400g, OR 2 CUPS:

100g butter
1½ tsp minced or very finely
    chopped garlic
400g chicken livers
2 Tbsp finely chopped fresh
    herbs such as thyme and
    oregano
2 Tbsp chopped fresh parsley
2 Tbsp Thai sweet chili sauce
¼ cup cream
2–4 Tbsp brandy or sherry (or
    a mixture of both)
freshly ground pepper
½ tsp salt

VARIATION: Serve the pâté before it cools and sets completely, as a dip for a selection of colourful, cold and crisp vegetables.

Melt the butter over moderate heat in a fairly large non-stick frypan. Stir in the garlic then add the chicken livers, straight from their pack.

Raise heat and cook chicken livers until no longer pink, turning frequently. For speed snip the large livers into much smaller pieces with scissors as they cook. Stir frequently adding the chopped herbs and chili sauce while livers cook. When cut surfaces are no longer red after 5–6 minutes the livers are cooked.

Add the cream, cook vigorously for about 30 seconds, then add the sherry and/or brandy and simmer for a minute longer. Turn off the heat, and add the pepper and salt.

Purée everything in the pan in a food processor while hot, then pour into a sieve. (A fine sieve produces the smoothest pâté.) For easiest sieving, bang the sieve on a fairly large bowl.

To cool the pâté quickly for immediate use, put the puréed mixture in a metal container and surround it with a mixture of ice blocks in cold water. Stir frequently for 1–2 minutes to remove the set mixture from the edges. When cold, transfer to serving bowl.

Let guests spread pâté on crostini, crackers, slices of French bread or other firm-textured, crusty bread. For contrasting colours and textures, serve carrot and celery sticks alongside if you like.

Blue Cheese 'Starters'

This smooth, well-flavoured mixture makes a basic "starter" which you can serve in different ways –

FOR CHEESE MIXTURE:
250g carton traditional cream
   cheese*
1 tsp onion pulp
1 tsp worcestershire sauce
   (optional)
1 tsp sherry
100g wedge (firm) blue vein
   cheese

FOR COATING:
½ cup finely chopped walnuts

FOR DIP:
sherry, cream or yoghurt

*Choose the firmest cream
cheese available. Softer
cream cheeses will be too
soft to use for a ball or log,
but will be fine in a lidded
container or for a dip.

(a) Form it into a ball and roll in finely chopped walnuts. To serve, surround the ball with crackers.
(b) Shape it into a cylinder and roll in chopped walnuts – this looks neater for longer!
(c) Press it into a container surrounded by crackers. This keeps well for a future occasion.
(d) Thin mixture with extra sherry, cream or yoghurt, to make a dip for vegetable crudités, potato crisps, crackers etc.

Spoon the cream cheese into a food processor or large mixing bowl in several blobs. Cut onion in half crosswise, and scrape the cut surface with the edge of a teaspoon to get onion pulp.

Add the worcestershire sauce (if using) and sherry. Break the wedge of blue cheese into the food processor bowl or coarsely grate it into the mixing bowl. Mix until blended.

If making a dip, thin to the consistency you want, as suggested above. Otherwise shape as suggested above. (If shaping a ball or cylinder, wrap the mixture in plastic film, shape, then chill it until firm before coating with the chopped nuts.)

Refrigerate leftovers (which are not covered with nuts or seeds) up to a week. (Coated mixtures are best eaten the day they are made.)

Hot Cream Dip

This hot dip turns any crisp raw vegetables into something special. Its original name, Bagna Cauda, translates as 'Hot Bath.'

2 Tbsp butter
3 cloves garlic, finely chopped
6 flat anchovy fillets
1 cup cream
crisp, cold vegetables*

*Suitable vegetables include carrots, celery, radishes, cucumber, snow peas, cauliflower, capsicums of any colour, small crisp lettuce or Belgium endive leaves, zucchini, young tender beans, asparagus, button mushrooms, and cherry tomatoes. Choose a colourful selection and keep the pieces small enough to be easily managed.

Although it contains anchovies, this dip does not taste fishy. (There is no substitute for the anchovies in this recipe - if you don't like the idea of using them, just forget about making the dip!)

The fastest way to make this is to have one person make the dip while someone else prepares a large platter of vegetables to surround it.

Melt the butter, add the garlic and cook over a low heat for 1–2 minutes. Add the chopped anchovy fillets and cream, then bring to the boil and simmer for 4–5 minutes or until it thickens slightly, mashing the anchovies as they soften.

Serve the Bagna Cauda mixture hot or warm. Stand a candle under a heatproof container of dip to keep it hot and liquid, or put it in a microwaveable bowl and remove it every now and then to 'zap' it in the microwave oven at intervals. (The mixture will probably be too thick to dip when cool.) Surround the dipping bowl with a large selection of colourful chilled raw vegetables cut into dipping-sized pieces. Make sure you have plenty of cocktail napkins to prevent drips of dip falling on the carpet!

Hummus

This is not a strongly flavoured, nor highly seasoned mixture, so is often eaten in larger quantities than many other dips or spreads.

300g can chickpeas
2–3 Tbsp lemon juice
1 large garlic clove, crushed
3–4 Tbsp tahini
3 Tbsp olive or other oil
liquid from can of chickpeas

NOTE: To make this dip without tahini:

Replace it with 1–2 teaspoons of Asian sesame oil.

OR add 2 rounded household tablespoons of peanut butter instead of tahini. Children often love this peanut butter version, especially with a couple of teaspoons of tomato sauce added for good measure!

OR if you have a spice grinder, grind about ¼ cup of lightly toasted sesame seeds and use them instead of tahini.

Drain the can of chickpeas, reserving the liquid. Put aside three or four chickpeas for garnish if you like.

Food process the rest of the canned chickpeas with the lemon juice, garlic and tahini until smooth, adding the oil in a thin stream. Thin it to the consistency of a spread or dip, with as much of the reserved chickpea liquid as you like.

Put the spread or dip in a small bowl, topped with the reserved chickpeas, and with a drizzle of olive oil or garlic-infused olive oil over it, if you like.

Serve with triangles of toasted pita bread, melba toast, crostini, crackers, or with a selection of raw vegetable crudités such as cauliflower florets, snow peas, carrots cut in strips or in diagonal slices, cucumber or celery strips.

NOTE: Tahini is a paste made from ground sesame seeds. Look for it in large supermarkets and stores that sell Middle Eastern foods. After opening, it may be kept in a cupboard for months, if not years. Stir the oil through the ground seeds before using it.

Mexican Cheese and Tomato Dip

This spicy and delicious hot dip is particularly welcome in cold weather. Buy twice as many corn chips as you think you will need, because they are likely to disappear really fast!

FOR 4–8 SERVINGS:

1 medium-sized onion, chopped
1 green pepper, chopped
1 Tbsp canola or other oil
1 tsp ground cumin
½ tsp ground coriander seeds
½ tsp smoked or plain paprika (optional)
1 Tbsp finely chopped jalapeno peppers (from a jar)
425g can chopped tomatoes
1 Tbsp flour
2 cups grated tasty cheese
¼ – ½ cup low-fat sour cream
coriander leaves or spring onions for garnish

Halve then peel the onion. Halve the pepper, and remove and discard all seeds and pith. Chop both into small (about 5mm) cubes. Cook these in the oil, without browning, for 3–4 minutes. Stir in the cumin, ground coriander and paprika (if using) and cook a minute longer.

Add the finely chopped jalapeno peppers, and 1–2 teaspoons of the liquid in the jar if you like an extra "tang" to this dip. Bring to the boil and add the contents of the can of tomatoes. (If you use a can of whole rather than chopped tomatoes, break them up.)

Toss the flour through the cheese, then stir into the hot tomato mixture until melted and smooth. Do not bring the mixture to the boil after the cheese has been added.

Serve hot, in a shallow dipping bowl, topped with sour cream and garnished with chopped coriander leaves or finely chopped spring onions. Serve surrounded by corn chips for dipping.

VARIATION: Make this dip without the green pepper if necessary. It is still very good! Replace ground coriander seeds with the same amount of dried oregano if you like.

NOTE: Look for pickled jalapeno peppers in jars in the Mexican food section of your supermarket.

Simple Salsa Fresca

This basic tomato salsa is best the day it's made, but can be refrigerated for 2–3 days.

¼ red onion or 2 spring onions, roughly chopped
1 large clove garlic (optional)
1 tsp wine vinegar or 2 tsp lemon juice
½ tsp ground cumin
¼ tsp crumbled dried oregano
4 large fresh red tomatoes, roughly chopped
pinch of chili powder OR finely chopped fresh chili to taste
2–4 Tbsp coriander leaves
½–1 tsp each salt and sugar

Chop everything in a food processor (or chop everything by hand), put in a bowl and stir together. Use the smaller amounts of salt and sugar and process until mixed but still chunky. Taste and add more salt and sugar to balance the flavours as you like them. Leave to stand for 15 minutes before using, if possible.

Use as a dip with corn chips, spoon onto crostini, alone or with other toppings, or mix with mashed avocado to make an easy Guacamole.

Guacamole

Guacamole makes a colourful, easy and popular dip, topping and sauce!

1 ripe avocado
2 Tbsp lemon juice or 1 Tbsp lime juice
1 finely chopped spring onion
¼ tsp salt
Tabasco sauce to taste
chopped coriander leaves (optional)

Halve the avocado lengthways, then scoop the flesh into a bowl, making sure to scrape out the greenest flesh close to the shell. Mash with a fork, and add the remaining ingredients, using quantities to suit your taste. Use immediately.

Use as a dip for corn chips, as a topping for Mexican foods, crackers or crostini, and in other ways you like.

VARIATION: Replace all the seasonings above with about ¼ cup of Salsa Fresca and fold it through the mashed avocado.

Quesadillas

Flour tortillas are a type of flat bread which may be turned into delicious, cheesy savouries, called quesadillas, in a very short time. Tortillas are thin, flexible and very versatile. (If you can't find "tortillas," look for other thin, flexible breads to use in the same ways.)

The tortillas may be crisped and their cheesy topping melted in a pan, under a grill or in the oven. Try them all three ways, to see which is fastest and easiest for you.

Flat Quesadillas

For flat (unfolded) quesadillas, brush outer edges (which will not be covered with cheese etc.) lightly with olive or canola oil.

Sprinkle the remaining surface with grated cheese. If you have time, chop several of the following into pea-sized pieces: red onions, olives, tomatoes, red or green peppers, brown flat mushrooms, avocado. Sprinkle these on evenly, add some canned Mexican bean mixtures and/or creamed corn and/or salsa if you like, then sprinkle a little more cheese on top.

Heat the tortilla flat in a heavy frypan, or grill it 5–8cm from the heat or bake it on an oven sheet at 180°C for 5–8 minutes. Cut in wedges with a heavy knife, eat as soon as the tortilla has browned and crisped, the cheese has melted, and other toppings are hot.

Folded Quesadillas

To make thin, cheese-filled crisp tortilla "sandwiches," lightly oil two flour tortillas. With the oiled side out, put grated cheese (and any extra flavourings suggested for flat quesadillas) between them. Cut into quarters before cooking, for easier turning and handling. Pan-cook, turning once, or grill, turning once, or bake (without turning) at 180°C for 5–8 minutes or until lightly browned and crisp.

Cut into smaller wedges soon after cooking, and eat while still warm and fairly crisp.

Eat just as they are, or as dippers, for guacamole and salsa.

VARIATION: You may find it easier to spread filling on only half of a tortilla which is to be cooked in a pan or under a grill. As soon as the tortilla has been heated enough to become flexible, flip the unfilled side over the filled side.

Chicken Quesadillas

Use cheese, a little salsa or chopped coriander leaves and chopped cooked chicken as a filling for folded quesadillas.

Spiced, Sugared Walnuts

These will keep for several weeks in an airtight jar.

2 cups walnut halves or large
   pieces
1 Tbsp egg white
½ cup icing sugar
1 Tbsp cornflour
½ tsp mixed spice
½ tsp salt

Turn oven to 125°C. Put walnuts in a bowl. Tip the measured lightly beaten but not frothy egg white onto the walnuts. Mix to coat thoroughly, using fingers. Sieve remaining ingredients into a shallow dish. Drop in the nuts and shake and turn them to coat. Arrange on non-stick liner or baking paper so they do not touch, and bake for 10–15 minutes until lightly browned and very crisp when cold.

Devilled Almonds

Heat these slowly so they don't brown before they heat through.

1 cup whole almonds
1 tsp sesame or other oil
1 Tbsp icing sugar
⅛–¼ tsp chili powder
1½ tsp each paprika and garlic
   salt
2 tsp Kikkoman soy sauce

Stir blanched or skin-on almonds and oil in a heavy frying pan to coat. Cook over low heat, stirring often, for 8–10 minutes, until a cut nut is very lightly browned. Mix the next four ingredients. Turn off heat, toss the hot nuts in the pan with soy sauce, then sift over the mixed seasonings and stir to coat. Cool. Store in an air-tight container for 1–2 weeks.

Devilled Popcorn

Spicy popcorn is very popular but is too "hot" for young children.

Mix dry seasonings as for Devilled Almonds. Heat ¼–½ cup popping corn in 1–2 tablespoons of oil in a large, lidded pot until popped, drizzle in another 1–2 tablespoons of oil then sieve in the seasonings, while tossing with a fork. Eat immediately or store in an airtight jar, for up to two weeks. (Yield is 4–8 cups.)

Dukkah

Dukkah is a highly flavoured mixture of nuts and spices. The crushed (but not powdered) mixture is made to suit individual preference, using what nuts and seeds are available and preferred.

FOR 2 CUPS:

½ cup sesame seeds
½ cup sunflower seeds
½ cup pumpkin seeds
1 cup blanched almonds
¼ cup cumin seeds
¼ cup coriander seeds
1 Tbsp (ground) paprika
1½ tsp rock salt
1½ tsp (ground) turmeric

olive oil for dipping
crusty bread chunks

Heat the oven to 180°C. Put the seeds and almonds in to roast, in separate foil dishes and/or pie plates, etc., in the order given. (We find that sesame and sunflower seeds take longer than the other nuts and seeds.) Watch carefully, checking them at least every 5 minutes, and take out each container when the seeds have darkened a little (but not a lot) and have an appetising aroma. (Most will take about 10 minutes.)

Leave the roasted nuts and seeds to cool, then grind with the paprika, salt and turmeric, in one or two batches in a food processor (using the pulse button), in a spice grinder or with a pestle and mortar. The mixture should have some texture - it should not be ground to an oily powder.

Serve Dukkah in shallow bowls. Let your friends dip pieces of crusty bread into good quality olive oil, then into Dukkah.

Store extra in airtight containers in a cool place, away from direct light. It will gradually lose its flavour on long storage, but is still good after a couple of months.

NOTE: Try using Dukkah in other ways too. It is good sprinkled on an oiled chicken before roasting, and sprinkled over plainly cooked vegetables such as green beans.

Marinated Feta & Olives

You can buy both marinated feta and different flavours of marinated olives but it is cheaper and far more satisfying to make your own – the results are impressive for very little effort.

FOR ABOUT 250g FETA (OR 200g OLIVES):

1–2 cloves garlic
1 small red chili
½ tsp black peppercorns
finely grated rind ½ lemon
few sprigs of thyme and
   rosemary, bruised
canola and olive oil, as required

VARIATION: Orange and Cardamom Olives: Use about 200g of mixed green and purplish (Kalamata) olives for interesting colour. Proceed as above, but using orange rind and 4-6 cardamom pods in place of the garlic, chili, lemon rind and herbs. Pour 1 Tbsp of orange juice over the olives before filling the jar with oil.

Cut feta into bite-sized cubes or chunks (2cm cubes are good). Peel and halve or roughly chop the garlic clove/s and de-seed and slice the chili. Put a layer of feta cubes (or olives) in the bottom of your jar. (Don't pack them in too tightly, or the flavoured oil won't be able to reach all the surfaces.) Add a slice of garlic, a couple of slices of chili, a few peppercorns, a pinch of lemon rind and a sprig or two of the herbs. If you want the jar to look its best, poke some of the chili, garlic and herbs down the inside of the jar (between the cheese and the jar) so you can see it easily.

Repeat this layering until you have used all the cheese (or olives) and/or filled the jar. Add any remaining seasonings (unless you are going to start another jar), fill two thirds to three quarters of the jar with canola oil, then fill to the top with olive oil making sure all the cheese (or olives) is/are covered. (Canola oil is a light, flavourless oil that will carry the olive oil flavours. You can use olive oil only if you like, but it is much more expensive and sometimes turns cloudy when refrigerated.) Put the lid on the jar and invert a few times so the oil and flavourings are mixed.

Leave to stand for at least 15 minutes before serving.

NOTE: These make good gifts too, but they are not really suitable for long term storage – keep them in the fridge and use within 7-10 days.

Antipasta Platters

Antipasta platters or selections always seem popular in restaurants and cafes – it's fun to have a whole selection of different things delivered to your table! One of the nice things about an antipasta platter is that it requires only last minute assembly, (or you can arrange one in advance and refrigerate until required). A simple trip to the deli or supermarket* can provide all you require. You'll be amazed how appetising and substantial a collection of 6–10 different items from the list of suggestions below (2–3 from each category) can look. You don't need much of any one item, 50–100g is usually plenty.

VEGETABLES, FRUIT & NUTS:

Olives: plain, marinated or stuffed (use 1–3 different types on a platter)

Marinated artichoke hearts (marinated ones have much more flavour)

Char-grilled capsicums

Marinated mushrooms

Pickled onions

Pickled walnuts

Sun-dried (or semi-dried) tomatoes

Pickled vegetables (carrots, cauliflower, etc.)

Gherkins/dill pickles

Caper berries

Basil and/or tomato pesto

Tapenade

Raw vegetable crudités

Grapes

Sliced kiwifruit

Melon slices, balls or wedges

Dried fruit and/or nuts

Sliced avocado

CHEESES:

Cubed feta, marinated or plain

Camembert or brie styles

Aged cheddar

Blue cheese (mild or strong to taste)

MEATS:

Ham, shaved or cubed

Pastrami, shaved

Prosciutto, shaved

Peppered pork, shaved

Sliced salami (a couple of different types)

Sliced bierstick, chorizo or other pre-cooked sausage

Pâté, bought or homemade

SEAFOODS:

Thinly sliced smoked salmon

Flaked hot-smoked salmon or other fish

Smoked (or marinated) mussels

Smoked octopus

Roll-mops

Rolled anchovy fillets

Sliced bread/crackers etc. to accompany

*****NOTE:** Some of these items are available bottled and/or canned on supermarket shelves too – they are ideal for keeping in the pantry.

Asparagus Rolls

Make these with lightly cooked fresh asparagus in season, and canned asparagus at other times.

Use fresh brown or white sandwich bread. Trim the fresh or canned asparagus stalks so they fit diagonally, corner to corner, across the bread. Allow 2 medium-thick stalks or 1 fat stalk for each slice of bread.

Boil trimmed stalks for about 4 minutes, until just tender and still bright green, then cool pot in cold water. OR put the cut lengths in an oven bag with 2 tablespoons of water. 16 medium-thick, cut stems usually weigh about 150g and microwave in 2 minutes on full power. Cool bag in cold water. Season with salt and pepper.

Cut crusts from sliced bread. Spread with softened butter flavoured with a little finely grated lemon rind. Place two medium stalks diagonally, top to tail, across bread. Roll up tightly, trimming off the inside corner for easier rolling. Roll finished asparagus rolls tightly in plastic film. When required, unroll plastic, cut rolls in half before serving.

Smoked Salmon with Horseradish

Cold-smoked salmon has a beautiful colour, delicious flavour and interesting texture. We always place it on top of savouries, where its colour will be most appreciated. Since it is very hard to cut thinly and evenly, we buy it already sliced, interleaved with plastic for easy handling.

TO MAKE HORSERADISH CREAM: Beat about 2 tablespoons of horseradish mixture (look for jars of grated horseradish flavoured with salt and sugar, since they have much more flavour than horseradish mayonnaise or dressing) with ½ cup of cream cheese until smooth. Taste and add more horseradish until it has the flavour you like.

Just before serving, spread it on the sliced crusty bread, then top with loose curls or folded strips of the cold-smoked salmon. Add a fresh herb garnish such as dill leaves, fresh fennel or chervil, and sprinkle with a few drops of lemon juice if you like.

Eggplant and Feta Rolls

It's hard to give exact quantities for this since everything can be varied to suit your own tastes, mood etc. If you are making them as a starter, look for smaller eggplants (about 6cm thick), or cut wider strips from bigger eggplants in half lengthways once cooked.

FOR 10-12 ROLLS (5-6 SERVINGS):

2 small – medium (about 400g total) eggplants
3–4 Tbsp olive oil ('plain', basil or garlic infused)
1 medium red pepper*
1–2 Tbsp balsamic vinegar
100–150g feta
about 2 Tbsp chopped basil (or 10–12 basil leaves)
salt and pepper to taste

*   If you are short of time, you can use bottled, char-grilled red pepper instead.

Cut the eggplants lengthways into thin (about 7mm) slices. Lightly brush both sides of each slice with oil. Place slices in a preheated contact grill (you may have to do this in several batches) and cook for 4–5 minutes on a high heat. OR arrange the slices on a non-stick sprayed baking sheet and place them under a preheated grill (5–7cm from the heat) and cook for about 3–4 minutes before turning and cooking a further 3 minutes. Set the cooked eggplant aside until cool enough to handle.

While the eggplant cools, prepare the remaining ingredients. If using a fresh pepper, cut the flesh from the core in flattish slices, brush these with any remaining oil and cook like the eggplant, then cut into 10–12 strips (you need the same number of strips as you have slices of eggplant). Cut the feta into the same number of fingers or slices too.

To assemble the rolls, lay a strip of eggplant on a board and brush lightly with balsamic vinegar. Lay a strip of red pepper and a piece of feta across one end, add a little chopped basil (or a basil leaf) then sprinkle with salt and pepper and roll up.

Arrange on a serving plate, drizzle with a little extra oil if desired and serve.

NOTE: If you want to serve Feta Rolls as a main course, use bigger eggplants cut a little thicker.

and Feta Packages

...ttle packages are loosely based on Greek Spanakopita – they look great ... effort. They can be served hot, warm or cold so really are versatile.

...TTLE PACKAGES:

1 Tbs...
1 medium on...n, diced
¼ cup pine nuts (optional)
200-250g frozen spinach,
   thawed and drained
100-150g feta cheese,
   crumbled
¼ tsp dried basil
¼ tsp thyme
¼ tsp freshly grated nutmeg
¼–½ tsp salt
black pepper to taste
1 large egg
8–10 sheets filo pastry
about 2 Tbsp melted butter or
   olive oil

Turn the oven on to preheat to 200°C.

Heat the oil in a medium-sized frypan, add the onion and cook until softened. Stir in the pine nuts (if using) and continue to cook until these are golden brown.

While the onion cooks, squeeze as much liquid as you can from the thawed spinach. Place the spinach in a large bowl and add the crumbled cheese, then the seasonings and the onion-pine nut mixture. (The quantity of salt required will depend on the saltiness of the feta – vary it to taste.) Add the egg and stir until well mixed.

Lay one sheet of filo on a dry surface and brush it lightly with oil, cover with another sheet, then cut crossways into 6 strips (each should be about 8cm wide). Place about 1 tablespoon of the filling mixture close to one end of the first strip, then fold the corner up diagonally to cover the filling (so the bottom edge meets the side). Keep folding the filling (straight then diagonally) until you reach the end of the strip. Fold any extra pastry under the package, brush lightly with oil or melted butter and place on a baking tray. Repeat until all the filling is used.

Bake at 200°C for 8–10 minutes until golden brown and firm when pressed in the centre. Serve hot, warm or even cold.

apped Savouries

...n little savouries made ...cut bacon slices around ...llops, plump prunes, ...mushrooms or inviting ...ple? Bake, grill or barbecue ...until the bacon is crispy and aromatic, and the filling is heated through but not overcooked.

The bacon should be thinly cut, with the rind removed. It should be streaky but not too fatty. Cut the rind off each slice with a sharp knife or scissors, then stretch the bacon lengthwise. (Before you cut each slice into shorter lengths, wrap one of the items you are going to roll up in the bacon, allowing a little overlap, so you get the length right.)

Pour water over the small wooden or bamboo skewers which you will use to hold the bacon in place, and prepare the food which is to be rolled.

Drain oysters and scallops on paper towels. Squeeze a little lime or lemon juice and pepper over them.

Pour boiling water over pitted prunes and leave to stand for 2–3 minutes, then drain and pat dry. Leave as they are or stuff each with a drained canned water chestnut, a walnut half, or a few pinenuts.

Cut the stems from cleaned button mushrooms. Sprinkle with a few drops of lemon juice and worcestershire sauce, and your favourite infused olive oil. Wrap up a sprig of thyme with each mushroom if you like.

Cut fresh ripe pineapple into chunky pieces. Sprinkle with angostura bitters and Tabasco sauce if you like.

Roll food up in the bacon, secure with the skewers and refrigerate until required. Preheat the oven to 225°C with the rack just above the middle. Bake the savouries on low-sided containers lined with sprayed foil, baking paper or non-stick liners. Make sure that edges are raised slightly so that cooking juices do not drip on the bottom of the oven. Bake for 6–10 minutes, until the bacon is lightly browned and the fillings just heated through or cooked.

Serve straight after cooking, with small paper napkins.

VARIATIONS: Grill or barbecue the savouries close to the heat for 6–8 minutes, turning to brown both sides.

Chili Cheese Mini-Muffins

These little muffins, made with strongly-flavoured cheese, fill the house with an irresistible aroma. For best flavour and texture serve them warm (but not hot).

FOR 24 MINI-MUFFINS:
2 cups (200g) grated tasty
    cheese
1½ cups self-raising flour
1 tsp garlic salt
2 Tbsp Thai sweet chili sauce
1 cup milk
1 large egg

Preheat the oven to 210°C. Use pre-grated cheese or grate it yourself. Measure the grated cheese, flour and garlic salt into a large bowl and toss gently with your fingertips to combine well.

Measure the Thai sweet chili sauce, milk and egg into a smaller bowl and beat with a fork until thoroughly combined. Pour the liquids into the dry ingredients all at once, then fold everything together, mixing no more than necessary to dampen the flour.

Using two dessertspoons, fill 24 mini-muffin pans which have been thoroughly sprayed with non-stick spray. Bake in the middle of the preheated oven for about 12 minutes, until the centres spring back when pressed and the muffins are golden brown. For easy removal from pans, leave muffins to stand 2–4 minutes before lifting out. (Some cheese may stick on the edges of the muffin tins. Remove it carefully.)

Serve warm muffins exactly as they come from the oven, on a folded serviette in a shallow basket or bowl.

OR cut a deep slash from the top, three quarters of the way to the bottom and insert a folded piece of cold-smoked salmon, salami, ham, cheese, a slice of a small tomato or a piece of roasted pepper, with a fresh herb leaf.

VARIATION: Add 2 tablespoons of chopped fresh herbs to the dry ingredients.

Smoked Salmon on Pesto Pancakes

It takes only ten minutes to mix and cook these herby little pancakes – but you may find that they are eaten in even less time than this!

FOR 24-30 PANCAKES, 5cm ACROSS:

1 large egg
½ cup milk
1 tsp sugar
½ tsp salt
1 Tbsp basil or dill pesto
1 cup self-raising flour

crème fraîche, sour cream,
    cream cheese or
    mayonnaise
thinly sliced cucumber
    (optional)
about 100g thinly sliced
    smoked salmon
chives, dill leaves, basil or
    parsley

Heat a large, non-stick electric or regular frypan.

Beat the first five ingredients in a medium-sized bowl with a fork until everything is blended.

Add the carefully measured flour, then mix again with the fork just until the mixture is smooth. (Do not mix more than necessary.)

Drop the batter off the end of a dessertspoon onto the preheated pan, twisting the spoon as you drop the mixture, so each pancake is as round as possible. Turn each pancake as soon as you see the first few bubbles burst on the surface. Cook the second side until the centre springs back when pressed lightly. If the surface of the pancake is too brown, or not brown enough when the first bubbles break, alter the temperature of the pan. If pancakes are too thick, thin the mixture with a little extra milk. If not serving the pancakes straight away, overlap the cooked pancakes on several layers of paper towel and slip them, towel and all, into a plastic bag to stop them drying out.

To serve, spread a little of any of the creamy mixtures on the pancakes. Add a slice of cucumber if you like, then add a slightly "gathered" piece of thinly sliced salmon and a sprig of whatever herb you choose. Cover with plastic film until the savouries are passed round.

Corn Fritters and Corn Cakes

These little savouries are called cakes if they are cooked as small pancakes on a lightly oiled pan or barbecue plate, and fritters if they are fried in teaspoon lots.

FOR ABOUT 36 CORN CAKES:

1½ cups cooked corn kernels*
1 large egg
½ tsp salt
¼ cup milk
for cakes add 2 Tbsp extra milk
    and 1 Tbsp oil
1 cup self-raising flour

OPTIONAL ADDITIONS:

½ cup chopped roasted red
    peppers
½ cup chopped ham or cooked
    chicken
2 Tbsp chopped fresh herbs

chili, tomato or other sauce for
    dipping

*Use thawed frozen corn kernels cut from boiled or microwaved fresh corn cobs, or a 425g can of whole kernel corn.

Using a fork, beat the egg, salt and first measure of milk in a medium-sized mixing bowl. Add two extra tablespoons of milk and the oil if you are making cakes, but not if you are making fritters. Stir in the (drained) corn. Add any of the optional ingredients if desired.

Sprinkle the flour on top of the corn mixture. Using the fork or a flexible stirrer, stir the flour through everything else until you can see no pockets of dry flour. Do not mix until smooth, since over-mixing makes the cakes (or fritters) tough.

FOR CORN CAKES: Drop teaspoon lots on a preheated, oiled pan or griddle. If mixture does not spread, stir in a little extra milk. Turn when the cakes are lightly browned on the underside and are firm enough to turn over easily. Press the turned cakes down so that more of their surface touches the pan. The second side is cooked when the centre springs back when pressed. (If the cakes are too brown, or not brown enough when the bubbles burst, lower or raise the heat. Cook only one cake at a time until you get the heat right.) Top warm corn cakes with a wedge of avocado or Salsa Fresca (page 17) if you like.

FOR FRITTERS: Cook teaspoonfuls in preheated canola or other oil at least 1cm deep, turning as necessary, until the crust is evenly golden brown and the centre cooked. Serve on cocktail forks or small skewers, with chili, tomato or other sauce for dipping.

Whitebait Puffs

Light, airy, with a delicate but recognisable flavour, these puffs make the most of a relatively small amount of Chinese whitebait – but you can use "the real McCoy" if you like!

FOR ABOUT 20 PUFFS:
150-200g (about 1 cup)
   frozen whitebait, thawed
2 large eggs, separated
½ tsp salt
1 Tbsp lemon juice
¼ cup self-raising flour
pepper to taste

Put a large, fairly heavy non-stick pan on to heat.

Run cold water through the whitebait in a sieve, then drain. Pick out any foreign bodies.

Break the eggs, putting the whites in a smaller bowl, and the yolks in a larger bowl. Add the salt to the whites and beat until they form peaks with tips which turn over at the top when the beater is lifted from them.

Mix the lemon juice, quarter of the beaten whites and the yolks, then stir in the flour. Stir in the drained whitebait, add remaining beaten whites, then fold everything together.

Drizzle a tablespoon of oil into the hot pan, tilt the pan so the bottom is covered, then drop dessertspoonfuls of mixture into the pan.

Cook until bubbles start to burst on the upper side of the puffs, then using a fork to stop the puffs sliding away, turn the puffs over with a thin, flexible blade. Cook the second side until lightly brown, then transfer to a plate in a warm oven until all the puffs are cooked. If the puffs are not light brown, adjust the heat when you cook the second batch.

Because the puffs are soft, place one or two (overlapping) on circles or ovals of French bread, or crustless rectangles of Vogels bread. Add dill or another herb and small lemon wedges for garnish, if you like. Serve as soon as possible after cooking.

Spicy Fish Cakes and Crab Cakes

Made with or without the addition of crab meat, these little cakes are always very popular. Add a topping, if you like, or forget about the topping and serve them with a dip instead.

FOR 16–20 CAKES:
2 thick slices of bread
½ small red onion or 2
    chopped spring onions
¼ cup roughly chopped
    coriander leaves, if available
1 large egg
about 2 tsp green curry paste
2 tsp fish sauce or ½ tsp salt
250g boneless, skinless fish
    fillets
100g surimi OR
    170g can crab meat OR
    100g extra fish fillets

Break the bread into several pieces and put in a food processor with the roughly chopped onion (or spring onions) and coriander leaves. Process until the mixture is finely chopped. Add the egg and curry paste, using more or less according to the spiciness you want. Add the fish sauce or salt and process briefly to mix.

Chop the fish into 1cm cubes and add to the processor. If you are making crab cakes, add the chopped surimi or the canned crab and the liquid from the can as well. Pulse in bursts, until fish is chopped in small pieces but is not puréed. (Under-processed fish will tend to fall apart in fingers when picked up, while over-processed fish turns tough and rubbery. Experiment, cooking a small amount of the mixture as soon as you think it is sufficiently mixed.)

Heat about a tablespoon of canola or grapeseed oil in a large, non-stick pan, form the fish mixture into bite-sized cakes, and cook over moderate heat for about 2 minutes per side, until lightly browned.

Serve soon after cooking, or reheat until warm in a microwave oven. If you like, top the hot or reheated cakes with a little sour cream or crème fraîche and a small amount of salmon caviar or lumpfish caviar. Garnish with dill or coriander leaves.

NOTE: We prefer the flavour of crab cakes made with surimi to that of crab cakes made with canned crab.

Rice Paper Rolls

These rice paper rolls are simple and delicious. For maximum ease just pick up half a cooked chicken at the supermarket as we have here.

FOR 12–20 ROLLS*:
1 clove garlic, chopped
1–2 tsp grated ginger
2 Tbsp each water, Kikkoman
   soy sauce and sherry
1 Tbsp brown sugar
½ tsp five spice powder
½ tsp cornflour

200–250g cooked chicken
   meat, shredded
12–20 rice paper wrappers
½ medium lettuce, finely
   shredded
1 medium carrot, grated
2–3 Tbsp chopped coriander
   or mint (or a mixture)
¼ cup chopped peanuts,
   optional
12–20 small spring onions or
   garlic chives, optional

*We use wrappers that are about 15cm across to make starter-sized rolls, but you can use bigger or smaller ones if desired.

Stir the first eight ingredients together in a small pot or microwave bowl, and heat to boiling (microwave for about 1 minute) until the sauce thickens and turns clear.

Place the shredded chicken in a small bowl, add the thickened mixture and toss to mix. (Store in fridge if preparing in advance.)

To make the rolls, soak the wrappers (3–4 at a time) in warm water until soft and white (about 20–40 seconds depending on the wrappers). Lift a wrapper out of the water, let it drain for a few seconds then lie it flat on a board. Place a little shredded chicken, some lettuce, carrot, a pinch of coriander and/or mint and a few chopped peanuts (if using) in the middle of the wrapper. Fold in the bottom and side edges to make an envelope shape, lie a spring onion or chive on top (if using), then roll up to make a little parcel.

Arrange completed rolls on a plate or platter, covering with cling film or a clean damp cloth if preparing in advance. Serve as is, or accompanied with a Vietnamese-style dipping sauce (combine the juice of 1 lime or lemon, ¼ cup each water and fish sauce, 1 Tbsp caster sugar, 2 cloves finely chopped garlic and 1 finely chopped small red chili, leave to stand for 5 minutes then serve).

Soy-Glazed Chicken Nibbles

In a microwave oven, these tasty chicken pieces can be cooked in a very short time.

FOR 4–6 SERVINGS:
500g chicken "nibbles"
2 Tbsp dark soy sauce or
⅓ cup Kikkoman soy sauce
2 Tbsp sherry
2 Tbsp brown sugar
about 1 tsp finely chopped or
grated garlic
about 1 tsp finely grated root
ginger
2 tsp sesame oil
1 tsp cornflour
2 Tbsp toasted sesame seeds

Put the chicken nibbles (individual chicken wing joints) in an oven bag then add all the remaining ingredients except the sesame seeds. Knead the bag gently but thoroughly to mix everything well. Fasten the neck of the bag with a rubber band, leaving a finger-sized opening so that the bag does not blow up like a balloon during cooking. Leave the pieces to stand in the marinade for at least 5 minutes before cooking.

To cook, lie the bag of chicken pieces and marinade flat on the floor of the microwave oven so the chicken pieces are in one layer. Check that the opening of the bag is not obstructed. Microwave on full power for 10 minutes, then flip bag over, and leave it to stand for 2 minutes. Pierce the thickest piece to check that it is cooked – if pink juice runs out, cook chicken for longer, in 1 minute bursts, until the juice from another pierced piece is clear.

Remove the cooked chicken pieces from the bag, sprinkle them with toasted sesame seeds immediately, then leave to stand for about 2 minutes, until the pieces darken and appear glazed. Pass small paper napkins around with the chicken, and eat with fingers while warm.

Oriental Meatballs

We sautéed, microwaved and baked these tasty little meatballs. Baked meatballs were easiest, sautéed meatballs looked best, but those microwaved were fine too.

FOR 48 SMALL MEATBALLS:
1 medium onion, chopped
2 cloves garlic
2–3 spring onions, sliced
¼ cup chopped coriander
   leaves (if available)
450–500g minced beef or
   pork
¼ cup fine dry breadcrumbs
1 egg
1 Tbsp cornflour
1 Tbsp each Kikkoman soy
   sauce and sesame oil
½ tsp salt
½ tsp sugar
2 Tbsp Thai sweet chili sauce

Serve on toothpicks, with your favourite dipping sauce, and with paper napkins to stop drips.

Put the first four ingredients in a food processor and chop finely. Add everything else except the chili sauce, then process in bursts until you get a smooth mixture which forms balls that don't break.

Divide mixture into eighths on a board, then divide each eighth into six even pieces. Roll each piece into a small ball and cook balls soon after shaping.

TO BAKE: Place the shaped balls in a large, shallow baking dish, on a non-stick liner. Bake at 200°C for about 12 minutes, or until a ball, cut in half, is no longer pink in the middle (brush with the chili sauce after 8 minutes).

TO SAUTÉ: Cook in a preheated, large, non-stick pan in a dribble of oil. Jiggle the pan while the balls brown, to keep them nice and round, then drizzle them with Thai chili sauce. Cover pan and cook for 2–3 minutes longer, until a cut ball is no longer pink in the middle.

TO MICROWAVE: Replace the Kikkoman soy sauce with dark soy sauce. Place half the balls in a circle around the edge of a microwave turntable. Brush with Thai chili sauce mixed with a teaspoon of dark soy sauce. Microwave uncovered, at full power, for 3–4 minutes. Stand for 1 minute then halve a ball to see if it is cooked through. If not, cook 1 more minute then test again. Cook remaining mixture in the same way.

Chicken & Mushroom Dumplings

Surprise and delight your friends with these delicious little packages!

**FOR ABOUT 30 DUMPLINGS/
DIM SUM:**

3 dried (shitake) mushrooms
2 Tbsp dry sherry
1 Tbsp Kikkoman soy sauce
2 cloves garlic
1 Tbsp finely chopped or
　grated ginger
1 egg
300g chicken mince
1 spring onion, thinly sliced
2 Tbsp chopped coriander leaf
about 30 sui mai or won ton
　wrappers (thawed if frozen)

soy and sweet chili sauce for
　dipping

Finely chop the dried mushrooms (from Asian food stores or some supermarkets), place in a small container, cover with sherry and soy sauce and microwave on high (100%) power for 1 minute (or bring to the boil on the stove top). Leave to stand while you prepare everything else.

Finely chop the garlic and place in a medium-sized bowl. Add the finely grated ginger, then the egg, and whisk lightly. Tip in the chicken mince, the sliced spring onion, chopped coriander leaf and the soaked mushrooms, then mix until everything is evenly combined.

Round sui mai wrappers (about 8cm across) from the frozen foods section of Asian food stores are ideal, but won ton wrappers (which can be found in some supermarkets) with the four corners trimmed off so they are roughly octagonal, also work well.

Place about a heaped teaspoon of the filling mixture in the centre of a wrapper, then gather up the edges and squeeze gently to form a "money-bag-shaped" parcel that is slightly open at the neck. Repeat until all filling is used.

Place the parcels in non-stick sprayed steamer baskets, 1cm apart. Cover and steam over rapidly boiling water for 7-10 minutes, until pastry is soft and filling is firm.

Serve immediately, with little bowls of soy and sweet chili sauce for dipping.

Thai-style Spring Rolls

These mini-spring rolls are delicious and remarkably simple to prepare as the filling requires no precooking, just a little assembly.

FOR 20–30 LITTLE ROLLS:

½ cup lightly packed rice vermicelli*

1 cup very finely sliced cabbage

1 medium carrot, grated

2–3 Tbsp roasted peanuts, chopped

1 Tbsp each oyster sauce, fish sauce and Thai sweet chili sauce

1 Tbsp chopped coriander (optional)

1 tsp sesame oil

¼ tsp each salt and sugar

20–30 (10cm square) won ton or spring roll wrappers

1 tsp cornflour mixed with 2 Tbsp water

soy and sweet chili sauce for dipping

canola or other oil for frying

Soak the noodles in warm water for five minutes while you prepare and measure the remaining filling ingredients into a medium-sized bowl. Drain the noodles well, then add them to the other filling ingredients and toss to mix.

Lie a wrapper on a board with a corner pointing towards you (like a diamond), then spread about 2 teaspoons of the filling in a line across the wrapper just below half way. (Don't be too generous with the filling, or you won't be able to fit it in!)

Fold the left and righthand corners towards the middle so the ends of the filling are covered, then, working from the corner near you, roll the wrapper up so the filling is completely enclosed. Seal the end by moistening the flap with a little of the cornflour-water mixture. Repeat this process until you have used all the filling mixture, or all the wrappers.

Heat the oil in a wok or small frypan and fry the rolls, five or six at a time, turning occasionally until golden brown. Drain the cooked spring rolls on paper towels and serve warm, accompanied with bowls of soy and sweet chili sauce for dipping.

*Very fine, clear-looking noodles (like threads of glass – they are sometimes called glass noodles) available from stores specialising in Asian foods, or larger supermarkets.

Crispy Wontons

Wonton skins are fun to fill and shape. Look for wonton skins in Asian food stores or large supermarkets.

FOR 40–50 WONTONS:
40–50 wonton skins
400g minced pork or chicken
1 Tbsp sherry or lemon juice
2 Tbsp Kikkoman soy sauce
1 Tbsp cornflour
1 tsp sesame oil
2–3 spring onions
2 Tbsp finely chopped
    coriander leaves (optional)

canola oil or other oil for
    frying
chili, tomato, or sweet and
    sour sauce for dipping

Thaw (wrapped) wonton skins if necessary. Put the minced pork or chicken in a bowl or food processor. Add the next four ingredients and mix with a fork or process to blend. Chop the spring onions and coriander very finely and mix them through the meat.

Tip the completed filling onto a board, divide it into four equal parts, then divide each part into 10–12 small blobs.

Before you shape the wontons put the oil on to heat. You need oil 2cm deep in a wok or medium-sized pot. It is hot enough when an unfilled skin turns golden-brown in one minute.

Take 4 wonton skins at a time and put a blob of filling in the middle of each. Dampen the skin surrounding the meat with a little water, then fold one edge over the filling, until it meets the other side, forming a triangle. Press the wonton skin together around the meat. Next, bend the folded corners towards each other, pinching them firmly together. (It doesn't really matter how you fold the wonton as long as the filling is completely enclosed.)

Lower the shaped wontons carefully into the hot oil, cooking two to four at a time. Turn them over if necessary. Cool cooked wontons on paper towels for a minute. Serve warm, with a sauce such as sweet chili sauce for dipping.

Crostini

Crostini are useful bases for many savouries, and good to serve with pâtés and dips.

Cut stale bread rolls or French bread crosswise or diagonally into 1cm slices. Brush with olive oil or spray with olive oil spray, and bake on baking paper or a non-stick liner at 150°C for 5-10 minutes until crisp and lightly browned. When cold, store in an airtight jar if you do not want to use them straight away.

For savoury crostini, instead of using plain olive oil, use a mixture of 4 parts of plain to 1 part of infused olive oil. Or add parmesan cheese, pesto, tapenade, ground cumin, mashed anchovies, etc. to the oil you are going to brush on the bread.

Published by
Hyndman Publishing,
PO Box 5017, Dunedin

ISBN: 1-877168-60-2
TEXT: ©Simon & Alison Holst
DESIGNER: Rob Di Leva
PHOTOGRAPHER: Lindsay Keats
HOME ECONOMISTS: Simon & Alison Holst
PROPS: Chrissy Doring
PRINTING: Tablet Colour Print

The recipes in this book have been carefully tested by the authors. The publisher and the authors have made every effort to ensure that the instructions are accurate and safe, but they cannot accept liability for any resulting injury or loss or damage to property, whether direct or consequential.

Because ovens and microwave ovens vary so much, you should take the cooking times suggested in recipes as guides only. The first time you make a recipe, check it at intervals to make sure it is not cooking faster, or more slowly than expected.

Always follow the detailed instructions given by manufacturers of your appliances and equipment, rather than the more general instructions given in these recipes.

Important Information:

For best results, use a standard metric (250ml) measuring cup and metric measuring spoons when you use these recipes: 1 tablespoon holds 15ml and 1 teaspoon holds 5ml.

All the cup and spoon measures in the recipes are level, unless otherwise stated. Sets of measuring cups make it easier to measure ¼ and ½ cup quantities.

Larger amounts of butter are given by weight. Use pack markings as a guide. Small amounts of butter are measured using spoons (1 tablespoon of butter weighs about 15 grams).

Abbreviations used:

ml	millilitre
tsp	teaspoon
Tbsp	tablespoon
g	gram
°C	Celsius
cm	centimetre

INDEX

Knives by Mail Order

For about 20 years Alison has imported her favourite, very sharp kitchen knives from Switzerland. They keep their edges well, are easy to sharpen, a pleasure to use, and make excellent gifts.

VEGETABLE KNIFE $8.00
Ideal for cutting and peeling vegetables, these knives have a straight edged 85mm blade and black (dishwasher-proof) nylon handle. Each knife comes in an individual plastic sheath.

BONING/UTILITY KNIFE $9.50
Excellent for boning chicken and other meats, and/or for general kitchen duties. Featuring a 103mm blade that curves to a point and a dishwasher-proof, black nylon handle, each knife comes in a plastic sheath.

SERRATED KNIFE $9.50
These knives are unbelievably useful. They are perfect for cutting cooked meats, ripe fruit and vegetables, and slicing bread and baking. Treated carefully, these blades stay sharp for years. The serrated 110mm blade is rounded at the end with a black (dishwasher-proof) nylon handle and each knife comes in an individual plastic sheath.

THREE-PIECE SET $20.00
This three-piece set includes a vegetable knife, a serrated knife (as described above) and a right-handed potato peeler with a matching black handle, presented in a white plastic wallet.

GIFT BOXED KNIFE SET $44.00
This set contains five knives plus a matching right-handed potato peeler. There is a straight bladed vegetable knife and a serrated knife (as above), as well as a handy 85mm serrated blade vegetable knife, a small (85mm) utility knife with a pointed tip and a smaller (85mm) serrated knife. These elegantly presented sets make ideal gifts.

SERRATED CARVING KNIFE $28.50
This fabulous knife cuts beautifully and is a pleasure to use, it's ideal for carving or cutting fresh bread. The 21cm serrated blade does not require sharpening. Once again the knife has a black moulded, dishwasher safe handle and comes in a plastic sheath.

COOK'S KNIFE $35.00
An excellent all-purpose kitchen knife. With a well balanced 19cm wedge-shaped blade and a contoured black nylon handle, these knives make short work of slicing and chopping, and have come out on top of their class in several comparative tests. Each dishwasher-safe knife comes with its own plastic sheath.

STEEL $20.00
These steels have a 20cm 'blade' and measure 33cm in total. With its matching black handle the steel is an ideal companion for your own knives, or as a gift. Alison gets excellent results using these steels. N.B. Not for use with serrated knives.

PROBUS SPREADER/SCRAPER $6.50
After her knives, these are the most used tools in Alison's kitchen! With a comfortable plastic handle, metal shank and flexible plastic blade (suitable for use on non-stick surfaces), these are excellent for mixing muffin batters, stirring and scraping bowls, spreading icings, turning pikelets etc., etc....

NON-STICK TEFLON LINERS
Re-usable SureBrand Teflon liners are another essential kitchen item – they really help avoid the frustration of stuck-on baking, roasting or frying. Once you've used them, you'll wonder how you did without!

Round tin liner	
(for 15-23cm tins)	$6.50
(for 23-30cm tins)	$9.50
Square tin liner	
(for 15-23cm tins)	$6.50
(for 23-30cm tins)	$9.50
Ring tin liner	
(for 23cm tins)	$6.95
Baking sheet liner	
(33x44cm)	$13.95

Prices as at 1 September 2001, all prices include GST. Please add $3.50 post & packing to any knife/spreader order (any number of items). Please note, Teflon prices include post & packing.

Make cheques payable to Alison Holst Mail Orders and post to:
Alison Holst Mail Orders
FREEPOST 124807
PO Box 17016
Wellington
Or, visit us at www.holst.co.nz